Sports Illustrated KIDS

SLAM DUNK

BOOK OF

BASKETBALL

by Matt Doeden

CAPSTONE PRESS
a capstone imprint

Published by Capstone Press, an imprint of Capstone.
1710 Roe Crest Drive
North Mankato, Minnesota 56003
capstonepub.com
SPORTS ILLUSTRATED KIDS is a trademark of ABG-SI LLC. Used with permission.

Library of Congress Cataloging-in-Publication Data is available on the Library of Congress website.
ISBN: 9781669068044 (paperback)
ISBN: 9781669068044 (ebook PDF)

Summary:
Everything you need to know about basketball in one book, written with voice, style, and authenticity for today's young fans. Created in partnership with elite sports magazine Sports Illustrated Kids, the evolving history, style, play, and players of basketball is presented through in-your-face graphics and fresh text. Full of action-packed photos, the Sports Illustrated Kids: Big Book of Basketball will have readers on the edge of their stadium seats until the final page.

Image Credits
Alamy: Historic Collection, 6, Hum Images, 7; Associated Press: 15, 74, 83, Alvin Chung, 22, Dave Tenenbaum, 60, John Locher, 42, 45, Marcio Jose Sanchez, 103, Nick Wass, 85 (2020s), 99, Pat Sullivan, 73, Steve Reed, 37, Stuart Ramson, 79, Ted S. Warren, 51, The Jefferson City News-Tribune/Jeff Haldiman, 81; Getty Images: Andy King, 88, Bettmann, 8, 11, Bryan Bedder, 105, FatCamera, 31, Focus On Sport, 85 (1970s), Jared C. Tilton, 54, Joe Murphy, 36, Kevin C. Cox, 107, Reebok/Neilson Barnard, 87 (bottom left), Rick Stewart, 61, Sports Illustrated/George Long, 16, Xinhua/Song Qiong, 34; Library of Congress: Frances Benjamin Johnston, 9; Newscom: Everett Collection, 12, Icon SMI/SI/Manny Millan, 25, Icon Sportswire/John Rivera, 50, KRT, 17, MCT/Akron Beacon Journal/Phil Masturzo, 97, MCT/Stephen M. Dowell, 13, MEGA/Goldin Auctions/Sotheby's, 21, Sipa Asia/Sipa USA, 53, Sipa/Laurent VU, 104, TNS/El Nuevo Herald/Hector Gabino, 46, Zuma Press/NurPhoto/Raddad Jebarah, 44, Zuma Press/Wolfgang Fehrmann, 48; Shutterstock: Africa Studio (blackboard background), 12–13 and throughout, Chamnong Inthasaro (basketball court background), 8–9 and throughout, ChromaCo (basketball player silhouette), cover (middle left), 1 (bottom left), 2 (top), Dan Thornberg (basketball texture), cover (middle) and throughout, EFKS, back cover, 1 (top) and throughout, Rawpixel, 27, SvgOcean ("basketball" word with silhouettes), cover (middle), 1 (bottom), teka12 (basketball player silhouette), cover (middle right), 1 (bottom right), vldkont, cover (bottom back); Sports Illustrated: Al Tielemans, 57, Bill Frakes, cover (bottom), 33, 80, Damian Strohmeyer, 85 (2010s), 87 (bottom right), 96, David E. Klutho, 29, Erick W. Rasco, 32, 38, 91, Hy Peskin, 85 (1950s, 1960s), 87 (middle left), John Biever, 78, John G. Zimmerman, 59, John Iacono, 85 (1980s), 87 (middle right), 89, John W. McDonough, 5, 66, 85 (2000s), 86, 93, 95, 100, Manny Millan, 18, 20, 24, 41, 62, 69, 70, 71, 72, 76, 77, 85 (1990s), 90, 98, 102, Neil Leifer, 65, Peter Read Miller, 63, Robert Beck, cover (top), 26, 43, 64, 94, SI Cover, 35, Simon Bruty, 39, Walter Iooss Jr., 19, 84

All internet sites appearing in back matter were available and accurate when this book was sent to press.

TABLE OF CONTENTS

Section 1: The Evolution of Basketball 4

Chapter 1: From Peach Baskets to the Modern Game. 6

Chapter 2: Changing Times, Changing Game 12

Chapter 3: Magic, Bird, and a New Game 18

Chapter 4: The Modern Game and the Rise of the WNBA. 24

Section 2: The Paths to Pro Basketball 30

Chapter 5: Learning and Building 32

Chapter 6: College Bound 36

Chapter 7: Preparing for the Pros 40

Chapter 8: Beyond the Big Leagues. 49

Section 3: Basketball Greats 56

Chapter 9: Game-Changers 58

Chapter 10: Raising the Game 68

Chapter 11: Legends of the Game 75

Section 4: Basketball Shoes, Shorts, and Style 82

Chapter 12: Fashion on the Court 84

Chapter 13: Personal Touch 90

Chapter 14: Expression on the Court. 96

Chapter 15: Fashion, Culture, and Social Issues 102

Glossary 108

Read More 110

Internet Sites 110

About the Author. 111

Index. 112

Words in **bold** are in the glossary.

SECTION 1: THE EVOLUTION OF BASKETBALL

Steph Curry spots up. He drills a long three-pointer. Swish! Sue Bird takes a bounce pass as she comes off a pick-and-roll. Zion Williamson soars through the air. He throws down a slam dunk.

These are the kinds of plays that bring basketball fans to their feet. The modern game is filled with fast-paced action. Yet for much of the sport's history, none of these plays even existed. There were no alley-oops. The game did not have **crossover** dribbles. There were no match-up zone defenses. It has taken nearly 130 years for the game to grow into what fans love today.

Golden State Warriors guard Steph Curry (#30) rises up to take a shot in a game against the San Antonio Spurs.

CHAPTER 1

FROM PEACH BASKETS TO THE MODERN GAME

Fans would barely recognize the sport when it was first played in 1891. Each team had nine players. They hurled a soccer ball at peach baskets. The baskets were nailed onto walls. Every time someone made a basket, they would have to climb up to get the ball out of the basket. The first games featured men. But women started playing the game less than a year later.

Dr. James Naismith invented the game of basketball in 1891. The early game featured peach baskets.

Naismith (middle row, right) poses with his first basketball team.

The early game was slow. Teams did not score many points. It probably was not much fun to watch. It is amazing that the game grew to become the popular sport that it is today.

Basketball first appeared in the Olympic Games in 1936. The U.S. men's team is pictured here.

Big Changes

The new game quickly grew popular. But it took time for it to look like the game that fans watch now. Backboards first appeared in 1895. Dribbling the ball became legal in 1901. At first, the rules allowed players only one dribble before they had to pass or shoot. That one dribble had to bounce over the player's head!

In 1936, men's basketball was at the Olympic Games for the first time. By this time, the game and rule book had **evolved** into something close to the modern sport. And yet, the game's evolution was just beginning.

COLLEGE BALL

The first known college basketball game was played in 1895. Teams from Hamline University and the Minnesota School of Agriculture in Saint Paul, Minnesota, faced off in the basement of Hamline's science building. The visiting team won, 9–3.

The first women's game came a year later. Stanford beat the University of California by the whopping score of 2–1!

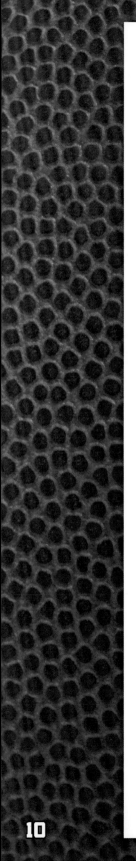

Jump-Starting the Game

Basketball in the 1920s was slow-paced. The game was a low-scoring grind. Players shot the ball from a flat-footed stance. The shots were easy to defend. Offenses struggled to score.

But all of that changed in 1936. Stanford player Hank Luisetti worked on a new type of shot. It would change the game forever. Luisetti's running one-handed shot was instant offense. It transformed the game almost overnight. The game's action was faster. The scores were higher. A new era of basketball had begun.

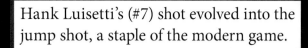

Hank Luisetti's (#7) shot evolved into the jump shot, a staple of the modern game.

CHAPTER 2

CHANGING TIMES, CHANGING GAME

College ball was the peak of the sport for many decades. That started to change in the 1940s. The National Basketball League was formed in 1937. The Basketball Association of America was formed in 1946. In 1949, the two pro leagues joined to create the National Basketball Association (NBA).

Center George Mikan was the NBA's first true superstar.

Stars drove the league from the very start. The first NBA superstar was George Mikan. He played for the Minneapolis Lakers. Mikan was big and strong. He dominated the game. The young league had to invent rules just to slow him down. For instance, the goaltending rule was made because of Mikan.

Goaltending, illegal in the NBA, is when a defensive player touches the ball while it is above the cylinder of the rim.

GOALTENDING

A rule barring defensive goaltending changed modern basketball. However, goaltending is legal in Olympic competition. The rule says that a defender cannot touch a shot that is on its way down toward the hoop. But the rule wasn't always part of the game. For more than 50 years, defenders were free to pluck away shots at any time. The new rule helped boost scoring—and excitement—in the game.

A New Wave

Basketball was changing. But so was society. Racism was a big problem in the United States. People of color were fighting for rights they had long been denied. Things slowly changed. That was true in basketball too.

In 1950, Earl Lloyd became the first Black player in the NBA. Lloyd broke the NBA's color barrier. He paved the way for future stars who would transform the league. Those players would spend decades fighting for equal treatment on and off the court. But the league was no longer limited to only white players.

Earl Lloyd (#11) was the NBA's first Black player. He helped pave the way for a new generation of basketball stars.

The Slam Dunk

The **jump shot** changed basketball in the 1930s. A new kind of shot made its mark in the late 1950s and early 1960s. It was the slam dunk.

Players had dunked as early as the 1940s. But the dunk became a force of the game when stars like Bill Russell and Wilt Chamberlain entered the league in the late 1950s. Their dunks rattled the rims. Dunks electrified crowds like no other shot. The game was played above the rim for the first time.

Wilt Chamberlain (13) dunking the ball

Bill Russell (left) and Wilt Chamberlain (right) battle near the basket.

Magic Johnson (#32) lofts a shot in a game against the Philadelphia 76ers.

CHAPTER 3

MAGIC, BIRD, AND A NEW GAME

In the 1970s, the NBA was struggling. Fans were drawn to college basketball, as well as other sports. The TV ratings were falling for NBA games. The league needed to be saved.

Earvin "Magic" Johnson and Larry Bird were the men to do that. Johnson and Bird had been **rivals** in college. They entered the NBA in the late 1970s. They brought a new swagger to the league. Their rivalry made the NBA more popular in the 1980s. Fans could not wait to see Bird's Boston Celtics play Johnson's Los Angeles Lakers. The TV ratings of these games soared. And a new era of the NBA was born.

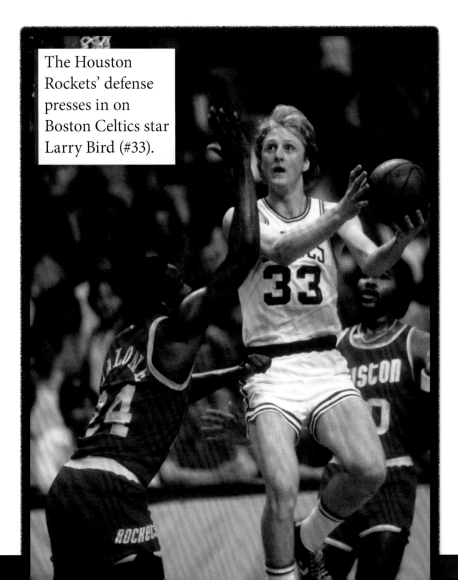

The Houston Rockets' defense presses in on Boston Celtics star Larry Bird (#33).

Air Jordan

Bird and Johnson may have saved the league. But another player took it to a new level. Michael Jordan had it all. He could drive the ball. He could step back and shoot from outside. He was **elite** on the defensive end too. Jordan was a big-time winner. He led the Bulls to six NBA titles in the 1990s. Fans loved him.

He had his own line of Nike shoes. He appeared in ads for everything from soda to underwear. Jordan's face was everywhere. The NBA's popularity grew and grew. For many fans, Jordan remains the greatest player ever to play the game.

Michael Jordan (#23) drives into the lane.

IT'S GOTTA BE THE SHOES!

No piece of sports fashion has made a bigger splash than Nike's Air Jordans. They were first released in 1985 with a price tag of $65. The shoe quickly became an iconic part of popular culture. Fans lined up to buy each year's new release. Even long after Jordan's retirement, Air Jordans remained one of the biggest pieces of basketball style in the world. In 2021, the sneakers sold for $170 for the basic sneakers up to $2,000 for specialty versions.

She Got Game

The men's game grabbed most of the headlines. But quietly, the women's game grew more popular too. A wave of female stars took over the college game. They did the same on **international** teams too. Cheryl Miller and Sheryl Swoopes thrilled fans. Fans loved to watch their slick ball-handling and dead-eye sharp shooting.

Several pro leagues for women came and went. But women were laying the groundwork. They were building a fan base. And something big was about to happen.

USC's Cheryl Miller (#31) was an unstoppable force in college in the 1980s.

CHAPTER 4

THE MODERN GAME AND THE RISE OF THE WNBA

Women's basketball was a huge hit at the 1996 Olympic Games. U.S. fans were excited as they watched Team USA win the gold medal. Their success caused NBA owners to form a new league. They created the Women's National Basketball Association (WNBA).

The U.S. women's team won gold at the 1996 Olympics, helping to ignite interest in women's basketball.

DID Y

In 2002

(#9) bec

woman

WNBA

The league began to play in 1997. Cynthia Cooper played for the Houston Comets. She and the team dominated the league early on. The WNBA game featured crisp passing and accurate shooting. The women showed strong **fundamental** play. Over the next three decades, the league grew. Stars such as Candace Parker, Maya Moore, and Sue Bird thrilled fans. They showed that the women's game was here to stay.

The age of the three-pointer

By the 2010s, the NBA was taking on a similar look. Powerful players such as LeBron James still ruled the court. But a new style was taking over. Pure shooters such as Steph Curry launched three-pointers at a record pace.

Steph Curry waits to show off his skills at the All-Star Weekend Skills Challenge.

Meanwhile, many NBA teams looked to **analytics**—the study of deep, detailed statistics—to drive the style of play. And the analytics were clear. Three-pointers and dunks were the most **efficient** shots in the game. The mid-range jump shot had been a big part of the game for decades. But a new way of playing had taken over. The mid-range shot was becoming a thing of the past. Teams around the league sought out the world's best long-range shooters.

NEW AGE STATS

For almost a century, basketball stats were about points, rebounds, and assists. But in the modern NBA, analytics has produced new, advanced ways to measure performance. New-age stats such as the Player Efficiency Rating (PER) and win shares (a stat that measures how much a player contributes to winning games) rate players on almost every move they make—from defensive ability to how they move without the ball. These new stats allowed coaches to find strengths and weaknesses that traditional stats didn't reveal.

Going Global

There were other changes too. For decades, players born in the U.S. dominated the NBA. But more international players were changing the face of the league. These players included Germany's Dirk Nowitzki, Greece's Giannis Antetokounmpo, and Australia's Lauren Jackson. The international players took the U.S. by storm.

The new wave of talent made the NBA and WNBA truly international leagues. They helped shift the focus of the game to a style built around the three-pointer. They have played a big role in the ever-changing style of basketball in the U.S. and beyond. Fans can only wonder what the game will look like in 20, 30, or 50 years!

Dirk Nowitzki (left, center) helped make the NBA a truly international sport.

SECTION 2: THE PATHS TO PRO BASKETBALL

The clock ticks down. The crowd roars. You're the star player on your high school basketball team. The game is on the line. You dribble and spin past your defender. You rise up to take the shot.

Cameras flash. College **scouts** watch from the stands. You know that this shot is just one step on your basketball journey. You have dreamed of a pro career from the time you first picked up a ball. You have spent your life playing street ball. You have gone to basketball camps. You earned your place on this team. And now, you want to show that you are ready for the next step.

You loft a shot. The ball sails through the air. Swish! It's good! You did it! But you still have a long way to go to get your dream.

A player launches a shot over his defender.

CHAPTER 5

LEARNING AND BUILDING

LeBron James. Michael Jordan. Sue Bird. It is a thing of beauty to watch the stars of the National Basketball Association (NBA) and Women's National Basketball Association (WNBA). But even the world's best ballers did not start out dropping dimes and draining threes. They had to learn the game. Players had to build on their natural talent. They spent hours on the court. They mastered their spin moves and sick crossovers.

DID YOU KNOW?

Only about 3 in 10,000 male high school players make the big time. That is a tiny 0.03 percent!

LeBron James (right) drives to the lane in a 2018 Eastern Conference Finals game against the Boston Celtics.

Tina Charles (#31) battles for position in the 2010 Women's NCAA Tournament.

TINA CHARLES: FROM THE STREETS TO THE PROS

Tina Charles played on the streets of New York City. But Charles wasn't that good at first. She didn't get chosen for pickup games.

That did not stop her. Charles kept at it. She got better. And better. Soon, she was ruling those pickup games. She was a star at the University of Connecticut. She later became a WNBA MVP. "If I'm going to be out there, I might as well be the best," she said. "And I think I'm close to that."

James Harden (right) leads drills in a camp for young basketball players.

The Basics

Young players work to get better. Basketball camps teach them the **fundamentals**. The kids play in local leagues and groups like the **Amateur** Athletic Union (AAU). These groups give players a taste of teamwork.

High school is where many players get a real chance to shine. High school basketball is big all around the U.S. This is where the world's best young players show their stuff for college and pro scouts.

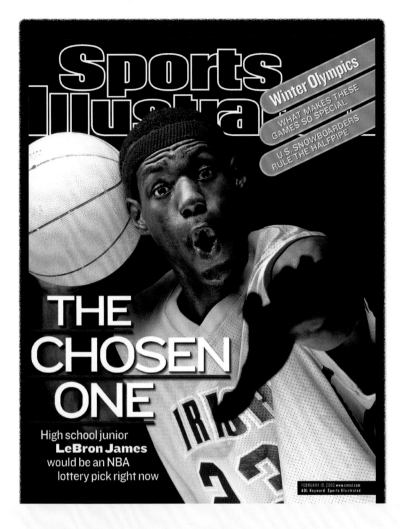

LeBRON JAMES: HIGH SCHOOL LEGEND

By the time he was 16, LeBron James was becoming a star. His size and skill made him a wizard on the court. James was on the cover of *Sports Illustrated* when he was 17 years old.

James went straight from high school to the NBA. At age 18, he was the top pick in the 2003 NBA **Draft**. He went on to become one of the greatest players of all time.

CHAPTER 6

COLLEGE BOUND

Most players go to college before the pros. There are some exceptions. But college is a must for many players. College coaches recruit the top high school players. Most give players scholarships. This is money for school and expenses. Players get this in exchange for playing on the team. Scholarships give players a chance to get an education. They can also show off their skills against the nation's best amateur players.

James Wiseman (#32) defends a player during his NCAA career with the University of Memphis.

BALLING OVERSEAS

LaMelo Ball took a unique path to the NBA. He left high school in his junior year to play in a pro league overseas. Ball chose to skip college. He starred on a pro team in Australia.

It was an unusual path. But it worked. The Charlotte Hornets selected him as the third overall pick in the 2020 NBA Draft. He was 19 years old.

LaMelo Ball shows off his new jersey after the Charlotte Hornets drafted him in 2020.

The College Game

Each college player has four years of **eligibility**. Some leave for the pros after just one year. They are often called one-and-done players. Others stay the whole time. They grow and build their skills in games and **tournaments**. If they are lucky, they get to play in the NCAA Tournament. It is a big-time competition. It is a chance to shine on the big stage.

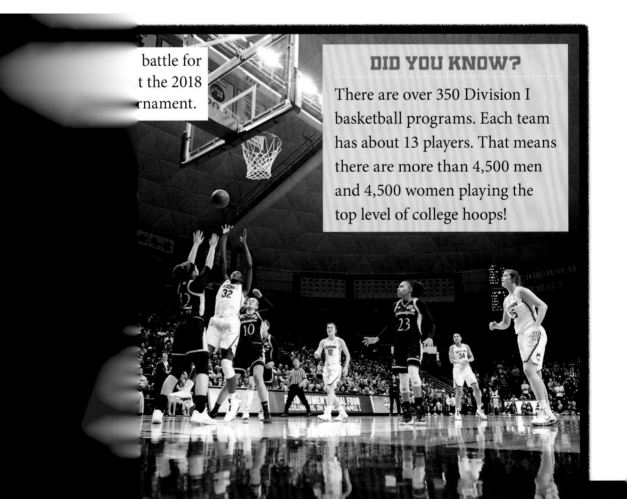

battle for t the 2018 rnament.

DID YOU KNOW?

There are over 350 Division I basketball programs. Each team has about 13 players. That means there are more than 4,500 men and 4,500 women playing the top level of college hoops!

Buddy Hield (right) tries to make a move against his defender in the 2015 NCAA Tournament.

BUDDY HIELD: GOING THE DISTANCE

Decades ago, most of the top players stayed in college for four years. But now, it is less common. Most top players leave after just a year or two.

Buddy Hield could have left the University of Oklahoma early. He would have been a high pick in the NBA Draft. But he stayed all four years. He was named the 2016 College Player of the Year. The New Orleans Pelicans picked him as the sixth pick overall in the 2016 NBA Draft.

CHAPTER 7

PREPARING FOR THE PROS

Once a player is old enough, he or she can enter the draft. It is a big deal to decide when to go pro. Players have to weigh a lot of factors. How high will they go in the draft? Is there a chance they will not be drafted at all? Could they improve their draft standings with one more year of college? And how important is finishing college to them?

Pro contracts can offer huge amounts of money. Players who stay in college have to wait for that payout. They could get hurt playing in college. That could ruin their chances of playing pro ball. There is no right answer for when to declare for the draft. Each player faces a different situation.

The Minnesota Timberwolves selected Kevin Garnett (left) fifth overall in the 1995 NBA Draft. Garnett skipped college to go straight to the pros.

Going Pro

Everything changes when a player decides to go pro. Their amateur careers are over. Now players can spend more of their time working out and training, in hopes of making a pro team.

The draft **combine** is a great chance for players to stand out. The combine is a giant tryout that takes place each spring. Players are measured. They do interviews. They perform drill after drill. Pro scouts track their speed. They watch the players shoot. They break down each player's skills. Scouts look at their passing ability and basketball IQ.

A player runs drills at the WNBA combine.

Russell Westbrook throws down a dunk
in a 2011 game.

Deni Avdija of Israel speaks to reporters after being selected in the 2020 NBA Draft.

The Draft

All the hard work leads to the big day—the draft. The WNBA drafts in April. The NBA usually drafts in June. The teams gather to pick players. They choose players round after round. The draft is a dream come true for some players. They wear the hats of their new teams. They talk to reporters. They meet their new coaches. It is a sad day for others. Those who are not picked face new choices. Is their dream over? Or do they need to find another way?

ERICA WHEELER: FROM UNDRAFTED TO WNBA ALL-STAR

The 2013 WNBA Draft did not go the way Erica Wheeler had hoped. No one chose the star guard from Rutgers. But she did not give up. She played overseas. A former player for the Atlanta Dream saw Wheeler play. Then she got a tryout with the Dream. She made the team. But she was cut after just one season.

In 2016, Wheeler signed with the Indiana Fever. She proved she belonged. She became an All-Star in 2019. She was named the All-Star Game MVP that year.

Erica Wheeler celebrates after being named the MVP of the 2019 WNBA All-Star Game.

Making the Team

Getting drafted is a big deal. But there is no promise of success. Most NBA and WNBA **rookies** have to work hard just to make a team's **roster**. They learn their teams' plays in minicamps. NBA hopefuls play in the Summer League. The league is loaded with many players battling for a roster spot. It is a chance for players to show their skills. They hope to prove that they belong on a team.

The last step is training camp. It is one final cram session before the start of the season. Rookies who make the cut have finally reached their dream. It's game time!

Chris Bosh (second from the left) and the Miami Heat prepare for the season at training camp in 2015.

CHAPTER 8

BEYOND THE BIG LEAGUES

Most young players dream of knocking down clutch shots in the NBA or WNBA. But not everyone can make it to the big show. So what happens when a player does not make a team? Is it game over?

No! The NBA and WNBA are the top leagues. But they are not the only ones. Players who do not make the cut can still play pro ball. And if they are good enough, they might have a chance at the top leagues down the road.

Many women play professionally overseas. This game features European teams TSV Wasserburg and Rutronik Stars Keltern.

The G League

The most direct path to the NBA is the G League. It used to be called the D League. This is the NBA's minor league. G League players do not earn huge **salaries**. They do not play in front of thousands of fans. Their games are not on national TV. But the G League is the first place an NBA team looks when they need to fill a roster spot.

Brantley (right) alt Lake City osts up against nder in this League game.

Alfonzo McKinnie (center) throws down a dunk during a 2018 pre-season game against the Sacramento Kings.

ALFONZO McKINNIE: G LEAGUE SUCCESS STORY

Alfonzo McKinnie wasn't on the NBA's radar when he finished his college career at Wisconsin-Green Bay in 2015. So McKinnie played overseas. In 2016, he tried out for the Chicago Bulls' G League team. He earned a spot. McKinnie did not waste his chance.

McKinnie went on to play with the Golden State Warriors. He was part of the Warriors team that went to the NBA Finals. In 2019, McKinnie signed with the Cleveland Cavaliers. He was then traded to the Los Angeles Lakers in 2020.

Playing Overseas

North America is not the only basketball hotbed in the world. Europe, China, and Australia have great pro leagues. Ricky Rubio, Yao Ming, and many other players starred in these leagues. Then they went to the NBA. Stephon Marbury became a star in China after his NBA career.

Many WNBA stars play overseas too. Maya Moore is famous for winning titles with the Minnesota Lynx. But she also won with teams in Spain, China, and Russia.

DID YOU KNOW?

WNBA players can earn anywhere from a base salary of $130,000 to about $500,000. But they can make millions playing overseas.

Stephon Marbury (right) directs the offense in this 2017 Chinese league game.

Paths to Glory

There are many ways to become a pro basketball player. Many players go the traditional route. They move from high school to college to the NBA or WNBA. But there are other ways to go. From street ballers to **international** stars, every player takes his or her own path. They use talent and hard work to chase their dreams.

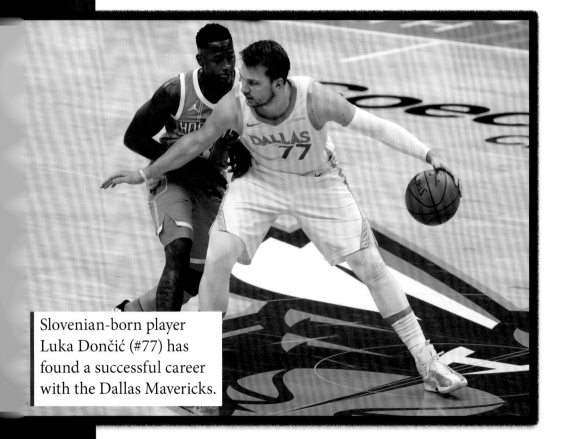

Slovenian-born player Luka Dončić (#77) has found a successful career with the Dallas Mavericks.

BASKETBALL PLAYERS BY LEVEL

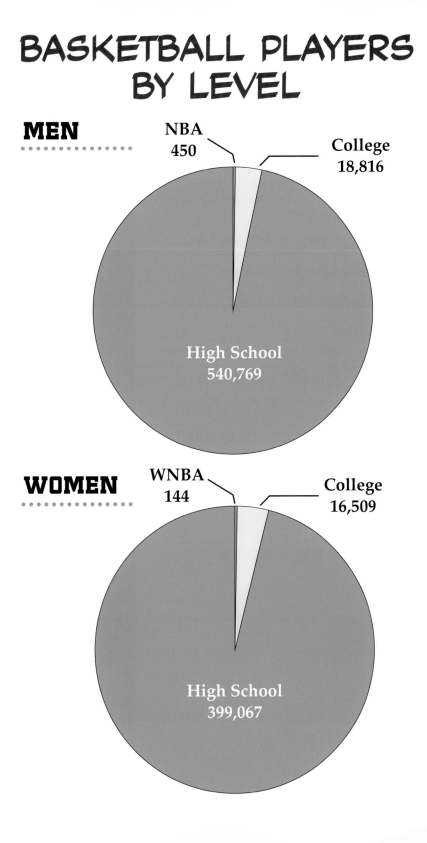

MEN

NBA
450

College
18,816

High School
540,769

WOMEN

WNBA
144

College
16,509

High School
399,067

SECTION 3:
BASKETBALL GREATS

The clock is ticking. It's a tie game in overtime. Steph Curry hurries the ball up the court. Three seconds remain . . . two seconds. Curry rises and launches a shot from deep. The ball sails through the air. Swish! Game over!

Curry is one in a long line of National Basketball Association (NBA) and Women's National Basketball Association (WNBA) legends. Their shot-making, passing, and defense have changed the way the game is played.

Sharpshooter Steph Curry rises up to take a shot in the 2015
NBA All-Star Game.

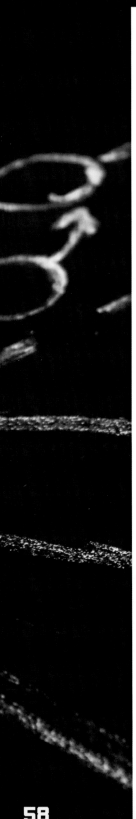

CHAPTER 9

GAME- CHANGERS

There are greats. And then there are game-changers. These are the players who altered the game itself.

Wilt Chamberlain

One of the first game-changers was center Wilt Chamberlain. He was 7 feet, 1 inch tall (216 centimeters). He towered over opponents. Chamberlain was a wrecking ball down low. He had power and **agility**, and he was willing to fight for the ball.

The NBA passed new rules just to slow down Chamberlain. They widened the lane near the basket. Players can pass through this area. But they can't stay there. The league was doing all it could to slow down Chamberlain's dominance.

Wilt Chamberlain leaps for a rebound in a game against the Boston Celtics.

Cheryl Miller (center) celebrates her Olympic gold medal with her parents in 1984.

Cheryl Miller

The women's game really began to take off in the 1980s. Cheryl Miller was a big reason. Miller was an amazing athlete with a sweet shot. She led the University of Southern California to championships in 1983 and 1984. She also won a gold medal with the U.S. team at the 1984 Olympics.

Miller was even **drafted** into the men's United States Basketball League. But knee injuries cut her career short. Fans can only wonder how much more she might have done if she had stayed healthy.

Cheryl Miller takes a shot in a game against the Texas Longhorns.

Kevin Garnett and Kobe Bryant

Until the mid-1990s, players usually didn't go straight from high school to the pros. But in 1995, high schooler Kevin Garnett changed that. The Minnesota Timberwolves selected him with the fifth pick in the **draft**. Garnett was a great athlete and a terror on defense.

...arnett (left) changed the NBA when ...e into the league straight out of high ...n 1995. The Minnesota Timberwolves ...him with the fifth overall pick.

Kobe Bryant (holding trophy) celebrates the 2010 NBA championship with his Lakers teammates.

A year later, Kobe Bryant followed in his footsteps. Bryant ended up with the Los Angeles Lakers. Bryant became one of the game's all-time **clutch** shooters. He won five NBA titles with the Lakers.

Dirk Nowitzki

In 1998, the Dallas Mavericks acquired German forward Dirk Nowitzki. At the time, few NBA players came from overseas. Many fans thought European players were not star-level players.

Nowitzki stood 7 feet (2.13 m) tall. He had great ball skills and a deadly shooting touch. Nowitzki changed the way people thought about European players. He also set a new standard in how big men could attack from the outside. He was the 2007 Most Valuable Player (MVP). He led Dallas to a championship in 2011.

Dirk Nowitzki (right) uses his long arms to defend the Lakers' Gary Payton.

The 1992 Dream Team included (left to right) Larry Bird, Michael Jordan, and Magic Johnson.

THE DREAM TEAM

Many experts credit the 1992 U.S. Men's Olympic team with helping to kickstart **international** interest in the game. The "Dream Team" included 11 future Hall of Famers. They included Michael Jordan, Magic Johnson, Larry Bird, and Charles Barkley. The team cruised to gold at the games in Barcelona. They thrilled fans with every pass, shot, and slam dunk.

Steph Curry (right) lofts a jump shot over Kobe Bryant.

Steph Curry

Steph Curry is an NBA game-changer. The three-point shot dominates today's NBA. Curry is better at shooting it than anyone.

In the 2012–2013 season, Curry made 272 three-pointers. It was the most in NBA history. But he was just getting started! Curry broke his own record in the 2014–2015 season and again in the 2015–2016 season. That season, he made a jaw-dropping 402 long bombs! His sharpshooting helped him win two MVP awards. He also won three NBA titles with the Golden State Warriors.

NBA AVERAGE 3-POINT SHOT ATTEMPTS PER GAME BY SEASON

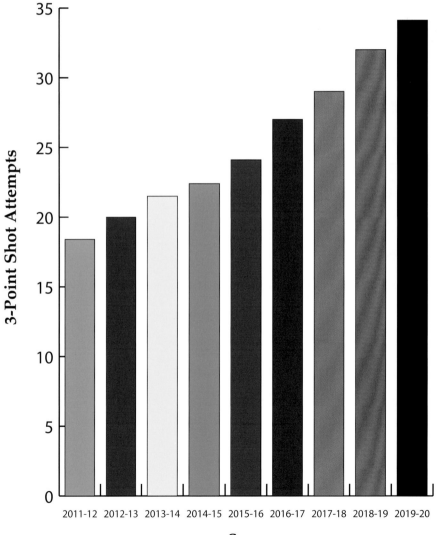

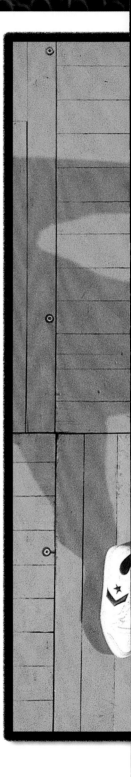

CHAPTER 10

RAISING THE GAME

Some legends just make people stand up and take notice. In the late 1970s, the NBA was struggling. TV ratings were low. Fans didn't seem interested.

Magic Johnson and Larry Bird

Two players changed all of that. Earvin "Magic" Johnson and Larry Bird were **rivals** in college. Once they arrived in the NBA, the league's popularity boomed. Johnson, of the Los Angeles Lakers, was a point guard in a forward's body. He was a wizard with the ball. He made crazy passes with ease. Bird starred on the Boston Celtics. He was a sharpshooting forward with a nose for the ball. The league's popularity surged when they faced off in the NBA Finals. They did this three times, in 1984, 1985, and 1987.

DID YOU KNOW?

The Lakers and Celtics are tied with the most NBA titles in history at 17 each. No other team has more than six!

Rivals Larry Bird and Magic Johnson battle for position in a clash between the Celtics and the Lakers.

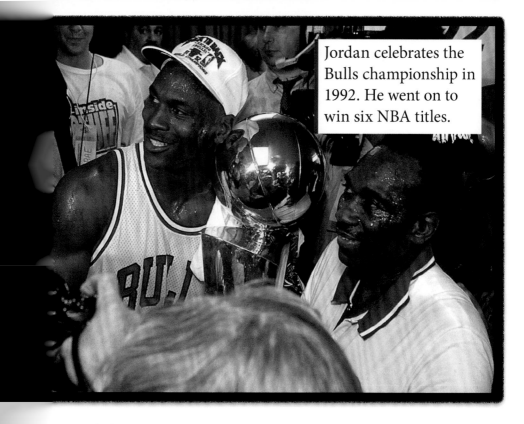

Jordan celebrates the Bulls championship in 1992. He went on to win six NBA titles.

Michael Jordan

Michael Jordan brought superstardom to a new level. He was a high-flying scoring machine and a shutdown defender. Nobody was better with the game on the line.

Jordan and the Chicago Bulls ruled the 1990s. They won three straight titles from 1991 to 1993. Then, Jordan shocked fans by leaving the NBA. He wanted to try a career in baseball. He came back in 1996 and led Chicago to three more titles. Jordan was an **icon** who was bigger than basketball. Most experts call him the best basketball player of all time.

DR. J

Before Jordan set the league on fire, Julius Erving was the game's most exciting player. His nickname was Dr. J. Fans plastered their walls with posters of his rim-rattling dunks. He made defenders look foolish in the pictures. Fans invented the term *posterizing* to describe it.

Julius Erving was a high-flying dunking machine.

Cynthia Cooper and Lisa Leslie

The NBA had Johnson and Bird. The WNBA had Cynthia Cooper and Lisa Leslie. The rivals were the two biggest stars in the league when it started in 1997. Their skills on the court helped the league grow into what it has become today.

Cooper, of the Houston Comets, could do it all. She was a great passer, shooter, and defender. She led Houston to the first four WNBA championships, from 1997 to 2000.

Lisa Leslie (#9) drives into the lane in a game against the Charlotte Sting.

Cynthia Cooper (front row, left) celebrates with her Houston Comets teammates after their WNBA title in 1997.

Leslie was a physical, athletic center. She was the first WNBA player to dunk in a game. She led the Los Angeles Sparks to championships in 2001 and 2002. The two stars paved the way for a new wave of modern WNBA players.

Bill Russell (#6) drives to the hoop in a game against the St. Louis Hawks.

CHAPTER 11

LEGENDS OF THE GAME

Some players just seem born to be great. They set the league on fire with their amazing skills.

Bill Russell

When it comes to winning, nobody can match Bill Russell. Russell joined the Celtics in 1956. He was the key to the greatest **dynasty** in NBA history. The 6-foot, 10-inch (208-cm) center was a force under the basket. He was also a great defender.

Russell won 11 NBA titles with Boston. That included eight in a row from 1959 to 1966. He even won two as a player-coach. He served as Boston's head coach and as its center from 1966 to 1969!

DID YOU

In 1966, Ru became Bos head coach. the first Bla coach in the He led Bost NBA title ir second seas

Diana Taurasi

Diana Taurasi is a winner. The 6-foot (182-cm) guard won three championships in college at the University of Connecticut. The Phoenix Mercury chose her with the first pick in the 2004 WNBA Draft. Taurasi didn't disappoint. She led the Mercury to WNBA titles in 2007, 2009, and 2014. And she became the league's all-time highest scorer.

Before becoming a WNBA star, Diana Taurasi (#3) helped the University of Connecticut to three NCAA titles.

UConn's Diana Taurasi (third from left) and teammates celebrate winning the NCAA trophy in 2004 after beating Tennessee for the title.

Taurasi is a big-time playmaker. She can score from inside and outside. She runs the offense and is a great passer. Many people call her the greatest player in WNBA history.

DID YOU KNOW?

Kobe Bryant was one of Taurasi's biggest fans. Bryant, nicknamed the Black Mamba, gave her the nickname The White Mamba. He said it was because she was so good in the clutch.

LeBron James

Most people call Michael Jordan the greatest player in NBA history. But LeBron James is a close second. James was drafted by the Cleveland Cavaliers straight from high school. His power and skill made him a force. He won **Rookie** of the Year in 2004 and became one of the league's best players.

LeBron James throws down a monster dunk in a game against the Detroit Pistons.

James can fill it up from inside and outside. And he's one of the best defenders in the league. The four-time MVP has also won four NBA titles. And he's done it with three different teams!

James (left) celebrates his 2004 Rookie of the Year trophy with Julius Erving.

Candace Parker

At 6 feet, 4 inches (193 cm), Candace Parker is a beast under the basket. She has the moves. She has the size to overpower opponents too. She's a force on the boards and a tough-nosed defender.

Parker came into the WNBA in 2008. She made a big splash. She won Rookie of the Year and MVP in her first season! Parker led the Los Angeles Sparks to the WNBA title in 2016. She also helped the U.S. Olympic team win gold medals in 2008 and 2012. The five-time All-Star remains one of the WNBA's greatest players.

Candace Parker (center) starred for the University of Tennessee before entering the WNBA.

Maya Moore (right) left the WNBA to fight for social justice. Here, she celebrates after helping free an innocent man from prison.

MAYA MOORE: MORE THAN JUST BASKETBALL

Maya Moore is a basketball legend. The Minnesota Lynx chose her with the first pick in the 2011 WNBA Draft. Moore was a key to the team's four WNBA titles over the next seven years.

Moore walked away from the WNBA in 2019. She wanted to focus on **social justice**. Her goal is to help reform the criminal justice system.

SECTION 4: BASKETBALL SHOES, SHORTS, AND STYLE

The arena was rocking. The fans were on their feet. The 1991–1992 season marked a new era in the history of the University of Michigan men's basketball team. Five of the nation's top college freshmen stepped onto the court together to take on college basketball. The "Fab Five" had the skills on the court. But they had something more. They had **swagger** and style.

The five young men came onto the court in very long, baggy shorts. That caught everyone's attention. Basketball shorts had always been shorter. Tighter. But not these. Their shorts kicked off a new wave of sports fashion. And the baggy shorts were the style of choice at all levels of basketball for nearly three decades. It was no longer just about playing well. It was about looking good while you did it.

Michigan's "Fab Five" included (left to right) Jimmy King, Juwan Howard, Chris Webber, Jalen Rose, and Ray Jackson.

CHAPTER 12

FASHION ON THE COURT

The Fab Five may have set a **trend** with their baggy shorts. But their style is just one chapter in the history of basketball shorts.

Early basketball shorts were . . . short. And tight. They mostly stayed that way until the 1980s. Then, a new wave of stars began wearing them just a bit longer. They were looser. Less restrictive. Less revealing. The 1990s brought on the ultra-long, baggy style. Men and women embraced it. But by the late 2000s, baggy was out. The shorts got just a bit shorter again.

Larry Bird (#33), sporting typical early 1980s short shorts, takes a shot over Julius Erving (#6).

BASKETBALL SHORTS TIMELINE

1950s

1960s

1970s

1980s

1990s

2000s

2010s

2020s

LeBron James dons his signature Nikes in a 2015 game.

Sweet Kicks

It's all about the shoes. At least that's what many basketball fans and players believe. No piece of basketball fashion is more important. Shoes need to give support, grip, and bounce. But they also have to look *good*.

Until the 1970s, the Converse Chuck Taylor was the shoe of choice. But then, a wave of new shoes changed the scene. The biggest of them was the Nike Air Jordan. It came out in 1985. The sleek, stylish shoes changed the market, on and off the court. Michael Jordan was the biggest star in basketball. And his shoes were iconic. Reebok Pumps were all the rage in the early 1990s. Nike, Adidas, and Under Armour shoes dominate the modern game.

BASKETBALL SHOES TIMELINE

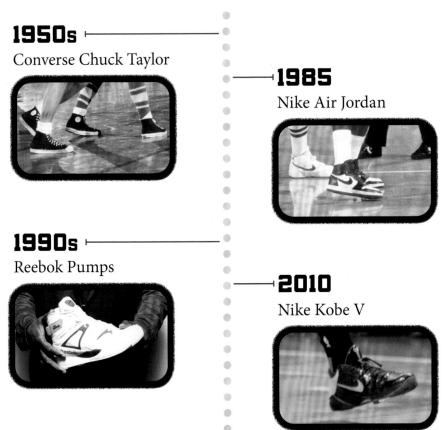

1950s
Converse Chuck Taylor

1985
Nike Air Jordan

1990s
Reebok Pumps

2010
Nike Kobe V

Accessorize!

On-the-court fashion doesn't stop with uniforms and shoes. Players have always added their own personal flair with **accessories**.

Wilt Chamberlain helped make headbands popular. Cliff Robinson, Candace Parker, and LeBron James all made the headband part of their style. Goggles and wristbands also added a personal touch. And who could forget high socks? Elliot "Socks" Perry got his nickname and basketball identity from his high socks. It's a signature style that's not for everyone. But when it works, it works.

Candace Parker rocks her headband during a WNBA Finals game against the Minnesota Lynx.

Kareem Abdul-Jabbar (#33) wears his trademark goggles as he battles for position near the basket.

CHAPTER 13

PERSONAL TOUCH

Style doesn't stop with clothes. A player's entire appearance can be a fashion statement. And for many, it starts with the hair.

In the 1990s, Dennis Rodman was almost as famous for his hair as he was for his basketball skill.

The **Afro** has been a staple of the National Basketball Association (NBA) for decades. From Dr. J to Ben Wallace, the Afro is a statement in big hair. Allen Iverson's cornrows and Brittney Griner's dreadlocks helped set new standards for style. Ricky Rubio's man bun, Michael Jordan's shaved head, and Sue Bird's ponytail all helped make their mark on the style of the game. And Dennis Rodman had a style all his own. His brightly colored hairstyles changed often. And they were *never* boring!

Brittney Griner (#15) plays against Spain in the 2016 Summer Olympic Games.

Well-Groomed

For men, hairstyle doesn't end with the head. Facial hair can be every bit as important to a player's look.

James Harden is one of the greatest players in history. But he's just as well known for his beard. It's quite a beard! In college, Harden played clean-shaven. But when he hit the NBA, he came with a new look. Harden started growing his beard in 2009. He's had it ever since!

Of course, he's not alone. Bill Russell, Kareem Abdul-Jabbar, and Kevin Love have all sported amazing beards. And Drew Gooden's braided beard was truly one of a kind.

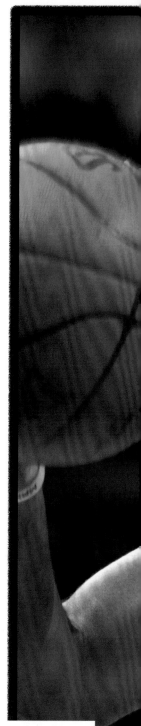

"The Beard," James Harden, gets his nickname from his bushy facial hair.

Got Ink?

Some style choices are forever. In recent decades, tattoos have become a big part of basketball culture. Dennis Rodman and Allen Iverson helped make body art popular. Now, it's everywhere. Crosses, phrases, and wild beasts cover the skin of many basketball players.

Kobe Bryant had "Vanessa"—his wife's name—tattooed on his arm. Cappie Pondexter has the Women's National Basketball Association (WNBA) logo. Seimone Augustus has a **sleeve** of flowers on her right arm.

Seimone Augustus (#5) shows off her sleeve of tattoos in a game for Team USA.

Chris "Birdman" Andersen set a new standard for tattoos in the NBA. He completed this punk style with a wild mohawk hairstyle.

BIRDMAN

Chris "Birdman" Andersen has some of the most famous tattoos in basketball. Andersen's many tattoos include wings on his arms and the words *FREE BIRD* on his neck. With his body art, wild hairstyles, and above-the-rim game, Andersen set a new standard for the punk style in the NBA.

Miami's Dwyane Wade performs his pregame ritual, doing pull-ups on the rim.

CHAPTER 14

EXPRESSION ON THE COURT

Style is about more than looks. It's about attitude. *Swagger.* Every player has his or her own way of showing their personality. It helps get them amped up. And the fans love it.

Rituals are a big part of it. LeBron James tosses chalk into the air before each game. Steph Curry shoots the ball from the locker room tunnel. Before he retired, Dwyane Wade did pull-ups on the rim.

Poof! A cloud of chalk dust floats through the air after LeBron James's famous pregame ritual.

Signature Moves

It takes a special player to make a signature move. Kareem Abdul-Jabbar had his famous skyhook. He would rise up and fling the ball over his head and into the net. Dominique Wilkins threw down amazing tomahawk dunks. He'd soar through the air and slam the ball down hard with one hand. Hakeem Olajuwon froze defenders with his Dream Shake. Maya Moore's spin move left defenders in the dust.

Kareem Abdul-Jabbar's signature skyhook was almost impossible to defend.

Elena Delle Donne (#11) fires a step-back jumper over Natasha Howard.

The list goes on. Earvin "Magic" Johnson was the master of the no-look pass. Elena Delle Donne and Dirk Nowitzki perfected the **fadeaway** jump shot. Each player's signature move became part of their style.

Celebrate!

Swish! How does a player celebrate big shots and plays? For many, it's just a shrug. But others have their own unique ways to pat themselves on the back.

Dikembe Mutombo was a shot-blocking machine. And he'd let opponents know about it. He used his famous finger wag. It was his way of reminding them not to try to shoot over him. Steph Curry celebrated big three-pointers by tapping his chest and pointing to the sky. Jason Terry would stick out his arms like wings and jet back up the court.

Jason Terry (left) jets up the court after knocking down a shot.

CHAPTER 15

FASHION, CULTURE, AND SOCIAL ISSUES

Shoppers line up for a chance to buy Nike Air Jordans in 2011.

Style doesn't stop on the court. NBA fashion is a part of popular culture. Air Jordan shoes are not just for basketball. They are a fashion statement. People line up to buy the new release each year. Basketball jerseys have become staples in hip-hop fashion. Some NBA fans even get tattoos like the ones their favorite players have.

Looking Good

Fashion is important to many players off the court. Designer suits, wild hats, and slick shoes help each player develop a style.

Russell Westbrook makes waves off the court with his one-of-a-kind fashion sense.

For many, a basic black suit is enough. But others dress to stand out. Russell Westbrook is a fashion trendsetter. His unusual combinations and bright colors keep people watching. The WNBA's Tamera Young has her own sense of style. It often includes designer clothing paired with bright sneakers. Swin Cash wows with sleek, elegant dresses.

Swin Cash shows off her sense of style in a blue evening gown at an event.

Style Sends a Message

In recent years, NBA and WNBA players have used fashion as a way to speak out on issues. In 2020, **social justice** was on many players' minds. Police shootings of Black people left some players wanting to speak out. Many NBA players wore the words *Black Lives Matter* on their jerseys.

The WNBA got involved too. Their warm-up shirts honored Breonna Taylor with the phrase *Say Her Name*. Taylor was shot and killed by police in March 2020. It was a small way that players could stand up for their beliefs and spread a message of change.

Players kneeled together before a 2020 NBA game. They wore T-shirts to raise awareness about social justice issues.

GLOSSARY

accessory (ak-SEH-suh-ree)—a stand-alone item that helps complete a style or look

Afro (AFF-roh)—a curly hairstyle in which the hair stands out all around the head

agility (uh-JIH-luh-tee)—the ability to move quickly and easily

amateur (AM-uh-chur)—a player who is not paid to participate in a sport

analytics (an-uh-LIT-iks)—the study of deep, detailed statistics, which is used to form strategies

clutch (KLUHCH)—important, game-changing situations

combine (KOM-byn)—an event where athletes complete tests to show their athletic abilities

crossover (KROS-oh-ver)—a dribble in which a player quickly changes direction by quickly dribbling the ball across his or her body

draft (DRAFT)—the system by which pro sports teams select new players

dynasty (DYE-nuh-stee)—a long period of dominance by a team

efficient (ih-FISH-uhnt)—productive and not wasteful

eligibility (el-uh-juh-BIL-uh-tee)—the amount of time a player can compete in college athletics, usually four years

elite (ih-LEET)—describes players who are among the best in the league

evolve (ih-VAHLV)—change over time

fadeaway (FAYD-a-way)—a shot taken while a player jumps, or fades, away from the rim

fundamental (fuhn-duh-MEN-tuhl)—a basic skill of a game, such as dribbling and shooting

icon (EYE-kon)—a symbol that stands for something bigger

international (in-tur-NASH-uh-nuhl)—involving more than one nation

jump shot (JUMP SHOT)—a basketball shot taken mid-jump

rival (RYE-vuhl)—team or player with whom one has an especially intense competition

rookie (RUK-ee)—a first-year player

roster (ROSS-tur)—all of the active players who make up a team

salary (SAL-uh-ree)—the amount of money players earn for playing a season

scout (SKOWT)—a person who evaluates basketball talent for college programs or pro teams

signature (SIG-nuh-chur)—something that sets a person apart and identifies them

sleeve (SLEEV)—a tattoo or series of tattoos that cover a person's arm

social justice (SOH-shuhl JUHSS-tiss)—the idea that society should treat all people equally and fairly

swagger (SWAG-uhr)—a highly confident way of looking and behaving

tournament (TUR-nuh-muhnt)—a sports competition that involves many teams and that usually lasts for several days

trend (TREND)—a popular movement toward a style or idea

READ MORE

Mattern, Joanne. *What It Takes to Be a Pro Basketball Player.* *Mankato, MN: 12 Story Library, 2020.*

Pryor, Shawn. *Basketball's Most Ridonkulous Dunks!* North Mankato, MN: Capstone, 2021.

Velasco, Catherine Ann. *Behind the Scenes of Pro Basketball.* North Mankato, MN: Capstone, 2019.

INTERNET SITES

NBA
nba.com/

SIKids Basketball
sikids.com/basketball

WNBA
wnba.com/

ABOUT THE AUTHOR

Matt Doeden is a freelance author and editor from Minnesota. He's written numerous children's books on sports, music, current events, the military, extreme survival, and much more. His books *Sandy Koufax* (Twenty-First Century Books, 2006) and *Tom Brady: Unlikely Champion* (Twenty-First Century Books, 2011) were Junior Library Guild selections. Doeden began his career as a sports writer before turning to publishing. He lives in Minnesota with his wife and two children.

INDEX

Abdul-Jabbar, Kareem, 92, 98
Andersen, Chris "Birdman," 95
Augustus, Seimone, 94
Avdija, Deni, 44

Ball, LaMelo, 37
Bird, Larry, 19, 65, 68, 69, 72
Bird, Sue, 4, 25, 91
Bosh, Chris, 47
Bryant, Kobe, 62, 63, 77, 87, 94

Cash, Swin, 105
Chamberlain, Wilt, 16, 58, 88
Charles, Tina, 33
Cooper, Cynthia, 25, 72
Curry, Steph, 4, 26, 56, 66, 97, 101

Delle Donne, Elena, 99

Erving, Julius "Dr. J," 71

Garnett, Kevin, 41, 62
Gooden, Drew, 92
Griner, Brittney, 91

Harden, James, 92
Hield, Buddy, 39

Iverson, Allen, 91, 94

James, LeBron, 26, 32, 35, 78, 79, 88, 97
Johnson, Earvin "Magic," 19, 65, 68, 72
Jordan, Michael, 20, 21, 32, 65, 70, 71,
    78, 87, 91

Leslie, Lisa, 72, 73
Lloyd, Earl, 14
Love, Kevin, 92
Luisetti, Hank, 10

McKinnie, Alfonzo, 51
Mikan, George, 13
Miller, Cheryl, 23, 60, 61
Moore, Maya, 81, 98
Mutombo, Dikembe, 101

Naismith, Dr. James, 6, 7
NBA Draft, 35, 37, 39, 44, 45
Nike, 20, 21, 87
Nowitzki, Dirk, 64, 99

Olajuwon, Hakeem, 98
Olympics, 8, 24, 60, 65, 80

Parker, Candace, 80, 88
Perry, Elliot "Socks," 88

Robinson, Cliff, 88
Rodman, Dennis, 91, 94
Rubio, Ricky, 91
Russell, Bill, 16, 75, 92

Swoopes, Sheryl, 23

Taurasi, Diana, 76, 77
Terry, Jason, 101

Wade, Dwayne, 97
Westbrook, Russell, 43, 105
Wheeler, Erica, 45
Wilkins, Dominique, 98
Williamson, Zion, 4
WNBA Draft, 44, 45

Young, Tamera, 105